D0468503

REAL WORLD MATH: HEALTH AND WELLNESS

COOKING BY THE NUMBERS

Cecilia Minden

Cherry Lake Publishing
Ann Arbor, Michigan

Published in the United States of America by Cherry Lake Publishing
Ann Arbor, MI
www.cherrylakepublishing.com

Math Adviser: Tonya Walker, MA, Boston University

Nutrition Adviser: Steven Abrams, MD, Professor of Pediatrics, Baylor College of Medicine, Houston, Texas

Photo Credits: Cover and page 1, © Tom Stewart/Corbis; page 6, Illustration courtesy of U.S. Department of Agriculture; page 25, © Richard Hutchings/Corbis; page 26, © Corbis

Library of Congress Cataloging-in-Publication Data
Minden, Cecilia.
Cooking by the numbers / by Cecilia Minden.
p. cm.— (Real world math)
ISBN–13: 978–1–60279–007–0
ISBN–10: 1–60279–007–8
1. Cookery—Juvenile literature. 2. Nutrition—Juvenile literature. I. Title. II. Series.

TX652.5.M55 2008
641.5—dc22 2007004669

Cherry Lake Publishing would like to acknowledge the work of The Partnership for 21st Century Skills.
Please visit www.21stcenturyskills.org *for more information.*

Table of Contents

CHAPTER ONE

Planning Ahead

What kinds of snacks do you keep in your refrigerator?

You walk in the front door after a swim meet, and suddenly you hear a low rumbling noise. Is it thunder? No, it's your stomach growling! All that exercise caused you to work up an appetite. Now you just have to answer the simple question, "What is there to eat?" When the hunger pangs hit, you want something fast! Do you grab a snack that is easy to make? Do you choose something healthy? With a little planning, you don't have to decide between these two categories. If you use your math skills and knowledge of a balanced diet, you can have a snack or a meal that is both **nutritious** and convenient.

Your task will be easier if you're aware of the different food groups and recommended serving sizes. The food pyramid at www.MyPyramid.gov places foods in the following categories: grains, vegetables, fruits, milk, meat and beans, and oils.

Grains are foods made from wheat, rice, oats, barley, and other whole grains. Vegetables can be fresh, frozen, canned, or dried. Whole fruits or 100 percent fruit juice are a part of the fruit group. Milk and products made from milk, such as yogurt and cheese, are in the milk group. Foods in the meat and bean group include meat (beef and pork, for example), **poultry**, fish, nuts, eggs, and beans (including black, kidney, and navy beans). The oils category features liquid oils such as olive and canola

Visit www.MyPyramid.gov to find out more about each food group and learn how to plan healthy meals.

oil, solid fats such as butter, and other foods high in fat content such as mayonnaise and salad dressings.

The Web site also includes information on serving sizes and how many servings you need from each food group every day. Experts say that an average 9- to 13-year-old needs 5 to 6 ounces (142 to 170 grams) of grain, 2 to 2.5 cups of vegetables, 1.5 cups of fruit, 3 cups (710 milliliters) of milk, 5 ounces (142 g) of meat, and 5 teaspoons (25 ml) of fat each day. These should be spread throughout the day. It is best to have three meals and one or two snacks.

You may be wondering how cooking food can possibly be quick or easy. How can you remember so many serving sizes? It often helps to think of common objects you can easily visualize in your head. For example, 1 cup of potatoes, pasta, or rice is about the size of a tennis ball. A 3-ounce

It is a good idea to have an adult nearby if you are using a sharp knife to cut vegetables or other foods.

(85-g) serving of meat is about the size of a deck of cards. A medium piece of fruit or 1 cup of leafy green vegetables is about the size of a baseball. A 1.5-ounce (42.5-g) serving of cheese is about the size of four stacked dice.

And 1 teaspoon (5 ml) of oil is about the size of the tip of your thumb.

Now that you know the basics of healthy eating you're ready to begin your work as a chef. Remember, it may be wise for an adult to assist you if you're using a hot oven or sharp kitchen **utensils**. Your math skills will come in handy, too. So what are you waiting for? Let's get cooking!

21st Century Content

If you want to be a smart chef, you need to be conscious of **calories** as you cook. The calories you **consume** when you eat food create energy that your body uses to function properly. Most 10- to 12-year-olds need about 2,000 calories a day. A very active person burns more calories than someone who is less physically active. What happens if you eat more calories than your body uses in a day? The extra energy will be stored as fat in your body, and you will gain weight. The nutritional labels on most foods provide important clues about how many calories are present in a single serving of a particular item.

CHAPTER TWO

Cooking with Care

Are you ready for that snack? It is time to get busy in the kitchen. A few simple safety rules and a little basic organization will go a long way toward making a meal that everyone will enjoy.

Always wash your hands carefully before you begin preparing food.

First, be aware that you and your family are not alone in the kitchen. You can't see them, but intruders called **bacteria** are present. They lurk on dirty counters. They cling to unwashed and undercooked food. Harmful bacteria can make you sick. They can also spread easily. Luckily, you can eliminate these germs. Just follow these four easy steps: clean, separate, cook, and chill. One of the most important ways to promote food safety is to regularly wash your hands. Clean them for at least 20 seconds in warm, soapy water before you begin cooking. Wash again after you finish handling different types of food. Wash your hands again when you're completely done working in the kitchen.

Be sure to clean countertops or surfaces that come into contact with food. Pots, pans, dishes, silverware, and any other utensils should be washed. Raw fruits and vegetables should be rinsed under cold water.

Firmer fruits and vegetables may even need to be scrubbed with a special brush. Cut off any bruises, soft spots, or brown patches that you find on the skin, or outer layer, of **produce**.

Keep eggs, fish, and meat separate from other items. If possible, use one cutting board for raw meat, poultry, and seafood. Use a different cutting board for fresh produce. Do not reuse any container that held raw eggs, meat, or fish without washing it in hot, soapy water.

Harmful bacteria die when food is cooked at the right temperature for the right period of time. Make sure you follow all cooking instructions exactly. You can find them on the food package or in a cookbook. Refrigerating or freezing leftover foods can slow the growth of bacteria. Your refrigerator should be set at 40 degrees Fahrenheit (4.4 degrees Celsius) and your freezer at 0°F (-18°C) to keep foods properly chilled.

Place leftovers in airtight containers with labels. Pack them in the refrigerator or freezer as soon as a meal is over. Check a cold storage chart. Learn how long you can safely store specific foods in both these locations.

REAL WORLD MATH CHALLENGE

Mai is helping her father prepare baked salmon for lunch. The recipe says to cook the fish at 350°F (177°C) for 40 minutes. They put the salmon in the oven at 12:03 P.M. **When should Mai and her father remove the pan from the oven? If they use a meat thermometer to check the temperature of the fish at 12:30 P.M., how much of the total cooking time has passed?**

(Turn to page 29 for the answers)

A responsible cook will not leave food safety to chance. Food must be cooked thoroughly. After all you do not want your cooking to make your family or friends sick. Even the best cooking instructions can sometimes leave you with questions. Some directions give you a range of cooking times. The cooking time might depend on what kind of microwave or oven you have. It might depend on the amount of food you are cooking. So how can you make sure your food gets hot enough to kill bacteria without overcooking it? Stick a meat thermometer in the thickest part of the food. Compare the temperature reading you receive with the temperature indicated in the cooking instructions. Now you know whether your food needs to cook longer or is ready to be safely served.

Always use oven mitts or potholders when taking hot foods out of the oven.

This may seem like a lot of information to remember, but every second of careful preparation will make your job as a chef easier. First, wash your hands. Then before you begin handling food, lay out all the containers, dishes, pots, pans, and utensils you need. Consider wearing an apron so you don't have to worry about staining your clothes. Let different members of your family help in the kitchen. This is a good way to save time and spend time together. Will you be working with sharp knives or boiling water? It might be wise to have an adult present. Always have potholders or oven mitts ready. You will need them when touching or lifting items that have been in the microwave or stove.

Above all, try to enjoy yourself. The more organized and relaxed you are, the better you can focus on safety and creating a nutritious, delicious meal for your family.

CHAPTER THREE

Do the Math: Calories Count!

Lasagna is a delicious dish that contains foods from the grain, meat and bean, milk, and vegetable groups.

Everyone in your family loves your mother's four-cheese lasagna with beef sausage. The treat just isn't complete without a basket of garlic bread. Don't forget the salad with creamy ranch dressing. You're thrilled when your mom asks you to help her prepare this dinner on Thursday, but you've also become more conscious about creating balanced meals. You don't want to overload everyone with extra calories. What simple cooking choices can you make that will result in the healthiest supper possible?

Consider using whole grain pasta and low-fat cheeses. Pick a low-fat salad dressing for your salad. How about using sausage made of ground turkey, which is leaner than beef. There's no need to skip the garlic bread, but keep an eye on serving sizes. Either have a single slice or split a slice with someone else at the table.

REAL WORLD MATH CHALLENGE

John is trying to decide which of three chicken recipes to make:

Recipe #1: Oven-fried chicken (350 calories)

Recipe #2: Oven-barbecued chicken (305 calories)

Recipe #3: Broiled chicken with honey (261 calories)

How many more calories do the first two recipes have when compared to the last recipe? Assuming that John normally burns off about 2,000 calories each day, what percentage of his recommended calorie intake does each of these recipes represent?

(Turn to page 29 for the answers)

Including many different kinds of colorful fruits and vegetables in your meals is an important part of healthy eating.

Remembering a few key terms can help you reduce calories. They will also help you get the greatest number of **nutrients** from the food you eat. Make an effort to cook with *whole grain* breads or pastas. Choose recipes that call for meat or fish to be *baked, broiled,* or *grilled. Fresh* fruit or vegetables or *steamed* vegetables are tasty sides. Be sure you select as colorful a variety of these items as possible. This insures you will be consuming a greater selection of nutrients. Choose *low-fat* when selecting salad dressings, frozen yogurt, ice cream, or milk. These cooking methods and ingredients are the best choices for a responsible chef who only feeds his or her family the healthiest foods.

REAL WORLD MATH CHALLENGE

Malcolm knows that portion sizes are an important way of controlling calorie intake. He understands that an occasional treat that's high in calories is okay as long as he doesn't go overboard. Once in a while he enjoys a single 250-calorie brownie. **How many calories would he consume if he ate the entire tray of 12 brownies?**

(Turn to page 29 for the answer)

CHAPTER FOUR

Do the Math: Conversions in the Kitchen

A breakfast casserole is made with eggs and may contain bacon, vegetables, potatoes, and other ingredients.

You want to try making a new breakfast casserole, but the recipe is for 16 people! Unless you have a very large family or really enjoy eating leftovers, you'll probably need to do some math conversions.

A recipe that serves a lot of people is great for a large dinner party but will need to be adapted if you want to feed just a few people.

First, be sure to read your recipe carefully. Look closely at the portion size and the number of people the recipe serves. Recipes usually feed an even number such as 4, 6, or 8. Determine how many people you want to feed, and try to figure an amount closest to that number. Next, put your math skills into play. If the recipe is for 12 people, but you're only serving

4, you can simply divide each ingredient by 3 (12 ÷ 4). If the recipe is for 6 people and you need to serve 17, round up to 18 and multiply each ingredient by 3 (18 ÷ 6). Knowing how to work with fractions is a big help when increasing or decreasing a recipe.

REAL WORLD MATH CHALLENGE

Annie wants to make chocolate chip cookies for a bake sale at school, and she needs to double her sister Maria's recipe.

Chocolate Chip Cookies (Maria's Recipe)

1 cup butter, softened

⅔ cup honey

¼ cup powdered milk

2 eggs

1 teaspoon vanilla extract

2 ¼ cups stone-ground white whole wheat flour

1 teaspoon baking soda

1 teaspoon salt

¾ cup chopped pecans

2 cups semisweet chocolate chips

How much of each ingredient will Annie need in order to double Maria's recipe? If Maria's recipe makes 36 cookies per batch, how many cookies will Annie have with a double batch?

(Turn to page 29 for the answers)

A set of measuring spoons is just one of the tools you will need when you cook.

Learning & Innovation Skills

What happens if you want to make a certain dish and discover that you are missing one of the ingredients called for in the recipe? Put your problem solving skills to work! You can often substitute one ingredient for another. Go online to a Web site such as www.foodnetwork.com to find substitution charts for common recipe ingredients. Many cookbooks also have substitution charts. When you become familiar with common substitutions, you can get creative and think up some of your own. They might not all result in food masterpieces, but trying out new ideas is part of the fun of cooking!

Think of all the ways that math plays a major role in figuring out cooking conversions. It is a good idea to have a calculator or multiplication

A calculator comes in handy when you are trying to increase or decrease the number of servings called for in a recipe.

cheat sheet handy in the kitchen. You can improve your math skills while you improve your cooking skills. After all, there are very few ways to be a talented chef without being a skilled mathematician!

Real World Math Challenge

Antonio is helping his father prepare a turkey for dinner. The cookbook recommends heating the poultry for 20 minutes at 325°F (163°C) per each pound of meat. **How long would it take Antonio to cook an 11-pound (5-kilogram) turkey? How long would it take him to cook a 6-pound (2.7-kg) turkey breast?**

(Turn to page 29 for the answers)

CHAPTER FIVE

A Family Affair

Preparing food can be a huge responsibility. It is also a lot of fun! You won't have a good time if you're stressed out or are trying to do too many things at once. So why not turn cooking into a family affair? Ask everyone

Cooking is fun when the whole family works together.

Young children can help by setting the table.

if they'd be willing to perform a specific task to help get ready for the meal ahead. Someone can dice fruits and vegetables. Someone else can work on preparing any meat, poultry, or fish. Perhaps one person can see to it that labeled containers are on hand so that you can quickly refrigerate or freeze any leftovers or unused ingredients. Another person can set the table.

Remember that cooking isn't simply another chore. When you prepare nutritious, tasty food, you're helping improve your family's overall health. Don't get frustrated if every meal doesn't turn out exactly the way you want. Becoming an expert chef takes patience and practice.

Sometimes meals won't turn out the way you plan!

Grab an apron and start cooking!

Your knowledge of the major roles that math skills and a balanced diet play in the kitchen will have you serving up delicious dishes in no time. So grab an apron and get busy—what recipe will you try today?

REAL WORLD MATH CHALLENGE

Ira knows it takes his parents about 40 minutes to clean up after dinner. He and his sister, Janice, go out after dinner to play baseball in the backyard, but Ira wishes they could have a family game. So he and Janice offer to lend a hand doing dishes, sweeping the floor, and wiping down surfaces that have come into contact with food. Sure enough, their contribution cuts the work time down to 15 minutes. **What percentage of the original 40 minutes does the new cleanup time represent?**

(Turn to page 29 for the answer)

Real World Math Challenge Answers

Chapter Two

Page 13

If Mai and her father put the salmon in the oven at 12:03 P.M. and need to cook it for 40 minutes, they should remove it from the oven at 12:43 P.M.

12:03 P.M. + 40 minutes = 12:43 P.M.

When they check the temperature of the salmon, 27 minutes of cooking time has passed.

12:30 P.M. – 12:03 P.M. = 27 minutes

Chapter Three

Page 17

The first recipe John is considering has 89 more calories than the third recipe.

350 calories – 261 calories = 89 calories

The second recipe he is considering has 44 more calories than the third recipe.

305 calories – 261 calories = 44 calories

If John normally burns off 2,000 calories each day, the first recipe represents 18 percent of his recommended daily calorie intake.

350 calories ÷ 2,000 calories = 0.18 = 18%

The second recipe represents 15 percent of his recommended daily calorie intake.

305 calories ÷ 2,000 calories = 0.15 = 15%

The third recipe represents 13 percent of his recommended daily calorie intake.

261 calories ÷ 2,000 calories = 0.13 = 13%

Page 19

If Malcolm eats the entire tray of 12 brownies, he'll consume a total of 3,000 calories.

12 x 250 calories = 3,000 calories

Chapter Four

Page 22

To double Maria's recipe, Annie will need to increase ingredient amounts as follows:

Chocolate Chip Cookies (Maria's Recipe)

1 cup x 2 = 2 cups butter, softened

$\frac{2}{3}$ cup x 2 = $\frac{4}{3}$ = 1 $\frac{1}{3}$ cups honey

$\frac{1}{4}$ cup x 2 = $\frac{2}{4}$ = $\frac{1}{2}$ cup powdered milk

2 eggs x 2 = 4 eggs

1 teaspoon x 2 = 2 teaspoons vanilla extract

2 $\frac{1}{4}$ cups x 2 = $\frac{9}{4}$ x 2 = $\frac{18}{4}$ = 4 $\frac{1}{2}$ cups stone-ground white whole wheat flour

1 teaspoon x 2 = 2 teaspoons baking soda

1 teaspoon x 2 = 2 teaspoons salt

$\frac{3}{4}$ cup x 2 = $\frac{6}{4}$ = 1 $\frac{1}{2}$ cups chopped pecans

2 cups x 2 = 4 cups semisweet chocolate chips

If Maria's recipe makes 36 cookies per batch, doubling this recipe will make 72 cookies.

36 cookies x 2 = 72 cookies

Page 24

At 20 minutes per pound, it would take Antonio 220 minutes to cook an 11-pound (5-kg) turkey.

20 minutes x 11 = 220 minutes

There are 60 minutes in 1 hour, so the 11-pound turkey will take 3 hours and 40 minutes to cook.

220 minutes ÷ 60 = 3 hours and 40 minutes

At 20 minutes of cooking time per pound of turkey, it will take 120 minutes to cook a 6-pound (2.7-kg) turkey breast.

20 minutes x 6 = 120 minutes

There are 60 minutes in 1 hour, so the 6-pound turkey breast will take 2 hours to cook.

120 minutes ÷ 60 = 2 hours

Chapter Five

Page 28

If it usually takes Ira and Janice's parents 40 minutes to clean up after dinner, 15 minutes represents 38 percent of the original cleanup time.

15 minutes ÷ 40 minutes = 0.38 = 38%

Glossary

bacteria (bak-TIR-ee-uh) tiny organisms often found on raw or unwashed foods that can lead to illness in people who eat them

calories (KAL-uh-reez) the measurement of the amount of energy available to your body in the food you eat

consume (kuhn-SOOM) take in

nutrients (NU-tree-uhnts) ingredients in food that provide nourishment

nutritious (nu-TRISH-uss) adding value to one's diet by contributing to health or growth

portions (POR-shuhnz) parts of something

poultry (POHL-tree) birds that are raised for their meat and eggs; chickens, turkeys, ducks, and geese are poultry

produce (PRO-doos) fresh fruits or vegetables that are grown on a farm or in a garden

utensils (yoo-TEN-suhlz) tools used for eating or preparing food

For More Information

Books

Gold, Rozanne, and Sara Pinto (illustrator). *Kids Cook 1-2-3: Recipes for Young Chefs Using Only Three Ingredients.* New York: Bloomsbury Children's Books, 2006.

Lagasse, Emeril, Charles Yuen (illustrator), and Quentin Bacon (photographer). *Emeril's There's a Chef in My Family! Recipes to Get Everybody Cooking.* New York: HarperCollins Publishers, 2004.

Ray, Rachael. *Cooking Rocks!: 30-Minute Meals for Kids.* New York: Lake Isle Press, 2004.

Web Sites

Home and Family Network—Cooking with Kids
www.homeandfamilynetwork.com/food/kids.html
Includes many recipes and cooking tips for parents and kids

U.S. Department of Agriculture—MyPyramid.gov
www.mypyramid.gov
For information on the various food groups and healthy eating

Index

About the Author

Cecilia Minden, PhD, is a literacy consultant and the author of many books for children. She is the former director of the Language and Literacy Program at Harvard Graduate School of Education in Cambridge, Massachusetts. She would like to thank fifth-grade math teacher Beth Rottinghaus for her help with the Real World Math Challenges. Cecilia lives with her family in North Carolina.